GW01606649
EVE

TWENTIETH CENTURY EVE

HEATHER DOUBLE

NOVA PUBLISHING LTD
Newton Abbot, Devon TQ12 4SG

First published 1990

ISBN 0 906330 27 0

Production & Printing in England for
NOVA PUBLISHING LIMITED
29 Milber Industrial Estate,
Newton Abbot, Devon TQ12 4SG by
Nuprint Ltd, 30b Station Road, Harpenden, Herts AL5 4SE.

CONTENTS

ACKNOWLEDGEMENTS

I wish to express deep gratitude to those who helped in the writing of this book.

My thanks go to Alf Cooper, a friend and fellow partner in the gospel who serves in Santiago, Chile, with S.A.M.S., and who encouraged me to put this into writing.

My thanks also go, for the valuable editorial comments and assistance in preparing the manuscript, to Tim Jones, Alan Penberthy, David and Fran Jutsum, Anne Double and Julie Noble.

I deeply appreciate my daughter Faith who faithfully served the family through the many hours that I was absent from household duties.

PREFACE

The basis of this book was initially taught as a seminar many years ago. When I was asked to take the seminar again, I began to search the Scriptures afresh on the subject. The more I sought, the more I found! As I counselled women after the seminars, I became aware of the need for more teaching in our churches and fellowships on this subject. I began to enquire and discovered that there were very few churches or ministries who were teaching real release to women.

Being an avid reader, I was also surprised to discover that none of the Christian women's books I read even broached the subject of our monthly menstruation and the related issues.

What I have written has come out of my own study of the Scriptures. I would like to emphasise here that to maintain any level of freedom in the Christian life we need to have faith in the cross of our Lord Jesus Christ. Alongside a faith in the cross we also need a faith in the working of God's Spirit. Both need to be a daily experience for all believers.

This book is offered to you with the prayer that each woman who reads it will be able to find a new dimension in her life which will, in turn, draw her closer not only to her heavenly Father, but also to her loved ones. Why? Because she will have found a new road to victorious Christian living and therefore be more effective for the kingdom of God.

Heather Double

Introduction

Years ago I heard a preacher beautifully illustrate the idea of redemption. I am sure many of you will also have heard the illustration. It was of a little boy who made himself a lovely yacht. He painstakingly rubbed and revarnished the wood many times, setting the mast, sails and rudder just right. One day, when he had considered his work well done, he took the yacht down to the lake to launch it. After he had played with it for many hours, the wind took the boat far out of reach, and the inevitable happened—he lost his prized possession. With much heartache he returned home believing, against all the odds, that the next day, or perhaps the day after, he would go down to the lake again and find his boat.

Many weeks passed and he had still not recovered his yacht. Then one day as he passed the local pawnshop, there, right in the middle of the shop window, was *his* yacht. Although by now it was rather battered and showed signs of being mistreated, he knew it was his.

Quickly he went into the shop to enquire the price. Running home he raided his money box, taking all that he had saved—for that was the price he had to pay to redeem his yacht. He ran back to the shop full pelt to buy his yacht.

Over the next days and weeks he spent all his spare time restoring his yacht to its former glory. The sail had been ripped, the rudder broken, the mast bent, the varnish was peeling. However, in what seemed like no time at all, it was fully restored.

This story is a picture of how we, as God's creation, have become battered and bruised. We have been mistreated by Satan and mankind. Now we need to allow the Spirit of God to recreate in our lives all that we should be. We take for granted that life as we know it is what God intended. But if we diligently search the Scriptures we will begin to realise that much of what we are today is not really as God planned we should be. In this book I wish to address an aspect of our lives as women which the Devil has taken advantage of and in which he has brought us into bondage, namely premenstrual tension and other related issues.

Chapter One

Is victory always short-lived?

As women we often find ourselves living in victory three weeks of every month, some of us perhaps only two weeks, then down we go, out for the count. We get defeated, depressed, dejected, moody, irritable with ourselves and with everyone else.

It then takes the next week to regain our composure and, with God's help, we live in victory again. But then the cycle starts all over again, month after month, year after year, with no hope of breaking free. Some have sought psychiatric help, or entered some mystical religion to find relief.

Our state of mind effects everything we do and everyone we meet. We cannot hide our true feelings from those around us, no matter how hard we try. Our moodiness and emotional temperature can easily be felt by those in our immediate circle.

I firmly believe that this is not the way God, our

Creator, intended us or our families to live. God's plan was for us to live victoriously 100 per cent of the time.

Ever since Adam and Eve's fall, women have lived under the oppression of their monthly menstruation. When God created us, with our monthly cycle, He intended us to live a balanced, victorious life.

We often complain that our menfolk do not have to cope with anything like this. I have heard some say, 'If my husband had to put up with what I have to every month then he'd be like me!' And after the birth of a child, 'If you had to give birth we would have only one child!'

No, the problem does not affect only us, it also affects those with whom we live. Our families have to try to cope with a wife, mother, daughter or sister who constantly seems to need to be wrapped in cotton wool and be treated very carefully in case her balance is tipped.

Did God create me to live under this strain?

> In the beginning God created us. After He had completed His work He looked at all that He had created and said that it was good, in fact very good (Gen 1:31).

This included us, with all our human emotions, body, soul and spirit.

'What happened?' I hear some of you say. 'I don't consider my monthly state to be good, let alone very good!'

What happened was *sin*!

Before Adam and Eve disobeyed God they were complete in every way. Sin entered their lives and because of this God said to the woman:

> I will greatly multiply your sorrow and your conception; in pain you shall bring forth children; your desire shall be to your husband, and he shall rule over you (Gen 3:16).

Do I have to live under the result of Eve's sin?

Contained in this verse is the start of our troubles. Ever since that day, women all over the world, in every generation, have felt the result of Adam and Eve's sin. What happened to Eve has been passed down from generation to generation.

I am sure you will be able to acknowledge this fact, probably saying, 'Yes, I can see that. What you are really saying is that I now have to live under the result of someone else's sin!'

Yes, but tell me this: when you read the New Testament, do you ever find that God expects us to live under the shadow of Eve's sin? On the contrary, when I read the New Testament it is clear that the Lord Jesus Christ came in order that we *do not have to live under someone else's sin.*

Did God curse Eve?

In Genesis only one creature was cursed because of Adam and Eve's sin—the serpent.

> Because you have done this, you are cursed more than all cattle, and more than every beast of the field; on your belly you shall go, and you shall eat dust all the days of your life (Gen 3:14).

> The Lord God commanded the man, saying, 'Of every tree of the garden you may freely eat; but of the tree of the knowledge of good and evil you shall not eat, for in the day that you eat of it you shall surely die (Gen 2:16–17).

Adam and Eve sinned; they ate of the tree of the knowledge of good and evil. This was in direct disobedience to God and the result of that sin was death in all mankind.

God's words to Adam and Eve in Genesis chapter 3 were only a statement of the consequences brought upon their lives for the sin of disobedience. God's pronounced judgement came as a direct result of sin. He made statements of facts to Adam and Eve of what was going to happen in their lives as a consequence of their sin. Bear in mind that Eve, up to this time, had not conceived nor given birth, so she had no comparison to make. What would happen in her life was a direct result of her own folly, but it would also continue from generation to generation. Death brought about by Adam and Eve's sin would continue, as would the consequences. The words God spoke as a consequence of their sin would become a curse upon women. There was now no way out for Adam and Eve or any of the men and women who would follow them. Death and its consequences for both men and women were to fall upon the whole of mankind.

Is there a way out?

What God said to Eve in Genesis 3:15 was a promise. He said to the serpent,

> I will put enmity between you and the woman, and between your seed and her Seed; He shall bruise your head, and you shall bruise His heel.

Through *her* seed (not through Adam's) a Saviour, a Deliverer would come and He would be able to revoke and reverse the events that had happened. Her 'seed' would bruise the serpent's head. Jesus, born of the virgin Mary, would destroy Satan's hold upon humanity.

God then went on to explain what Eve's seed would redeem her from. He did not say that she *must* have pain to conceive and bring children to birth, but that she *would*. Also, that her desire *would* be towards her husband and that he *would* rule over her. A statement of clear fact. He did not say that men *must* rule over women, just that they *would*.

From this time on Satan would so twist the sinful nature of man that men would want to dominate and rule women. Satan would take advantage of the situation of sin and its consequences to allow the domination of women by men to continue throughout history.

Chapter Two

Good news!

> For as many as are of the works of the law are under the curse; for it is written, 'Cursed is everyone who does not continue in all things which are written in the book of the law, to do them.' But that no one is justified by the law in the sight of God is evident, for 'The just shall live by faith.' Yet the law is not of faith, but 'The man who does them shall live by them.' Christ has redeemed us from the curse of the law, having become a curse for us (for it is written, 'Cursed is everyone who hangs on a tree'), that the blessing of Abraham might come upon the Gentiles in Christ Jesus, that we might receive the promise of the Spirit through faith (Gal 3:10–14).

Did you notice verse 13: *Christ has redeemed us from the curse of the law?*

The law referred to here consists mainly of two parts: first, the Old Testament rituals of the Tabernacle, its sacrifices, and priesthood; second, the Ten Commandments and laws of hygiene, with all their dos and don'ts, given to Moses on Mount Sinai.

In verse 24 of Galatians chapter 3 Paul tells us that 'the law was a schoolmaster (or tutor) to bring us to Christ, that we might be justified by faith'. The word translated here to mean 'schoolmaster' is unfortunately misleading to us in the Western world. In the Roman world of the New Testament the 'pedagogue' was, in fact, not an actual teacher, but a slave whose duty it was to take the child to school; he was a guardian until the child was old enough to legally become a son. In the same way, once faith has come, we are no longer under a 'pedagogue' (schoolmaster). We become children and legally free from the 'pedagogue' (schoolmaster) by faith in Jesus Christ. The law was simply a means to take us to the place we should have been in; namely, living to the standard God required. Therefore, Jesus came to fulfil the law and give us freedom from having to strive to keep the law. The law will always bring us to face death or life and we have to make the choice. We have to choose life if we are to live to God's standard.

Deuteronomy 30:19–20 provides us with a clear view of the choice Moses gave to the children of Israel.

> I call heaven and earth as witnesses today against you, that I have set before you life and death, blessing and cursing; therefore choose life, that both you and your descendants may live; that you

> may love the Lord your God, that you may obey His voice, and that you may cling to Him, for He is your life and the length of your days.

We couldn't set ourselves free from the curse of the law by simply keeping the law, but Jesus, through fulfilling the law and dying in our place, has set us free from that curse. I believe that the same principle applies to any curse or bondage brought to us through sin. We can claim freedom from any curse in our lives, no matter what brought it—whether it came from occult practice through our ancestors, from our own personal involvement, or perhaps by some other means.

It is interesting to discover the meaning of the word 'curse'. One definition is 'being hemmed in by obstacles and being powerless to resist'. It has also been explained as being bound by a spell. As we look into the consequences of death which came because of sin, we will see that they have become as a curse in our lives. Many women even refer to their monthly menstruation as 'a curse'; for some women it has become in reality 'a curse' and they feel in complete bondage to their monthly cycle. To be 'hemmed in by obstacles' is truly a definition of what has happened to us as women. There are obstacles placed around our lives over which we appear to have no control. We are powerless to resist these obstacles until we come to the cross of the Lord Jesus Christ and recognise what has happened.

The great exchange

Romans 5:12–21 reads:

> Therefore, just as through one man sin entered the world, and death through sin, and thus death spread to all men, because all sinned—(For until the law sin was in the world, but sin is not imputed when there is no law. Nevertheless death reigned from Adam to Moses, even over those who had not sinned according to the likeness of the transgression of Adam, who is a type of Him who was to come. But the free gift is not like the offence. For if by one man's offence many died, much more the grace of God and the gift by the grace of the one Man, Jesus Christ, abounded to many. And the gift is not like that which came through the one who sinned. For the judgment which came from one offence resulted in condemnation, but the free gift which came from many offences resulted in justification. For if by the one man's offence death reigned through the one, much more those who receive abundance of grace and of the gift of righteousness will reign in life through the One, Jesus Christ.)
>
> Therefore, as through one man's offence judgment came to all men, resulting in condemnation, even so through one Man's righteous act the free gift came to all men, resulting in justification of life. For as by one man's disobedience many were made sinners, so also by one Man's obedience many will be made righteous. Moreover the law entered that the offence might abound. But where sin abounded, grace abounded much more, so that as sin reigned in death, even so grace might reign through righteousness to eternal life through Jesus Christ our Lord.

The exchange is obvious! Because of one man's disobedience, death entered the world but now, because of another man's obedience, life would come to all mankind! We exchange the judgement of death for the abundance of God's grace. The Lord Jesus Christ was made a curse for us upon the cross in order that we might receive blessing.

If we have any problems in our life there is only one place to which we can go to find God's provision—*the cross*; and to the One who died upon it—Jesus Christ Himself!

Through what Jesus Christ accomplished by His death upon the cross every provision of God has been made available to us. Spiritual, physical and material provision has been made available to us (see 2 Corinthians 8:9; Isaiah 53:4–5; 1 Peter 1:3–5; Luke 12:31; 2 Corinthians 9:8–15). It is only through the cross that we can come to God and receive His provisions and blessings.

Colossians 1:19–20 says:

> For it pleased the Father that in Him [Jesus Christ] all the fullness should dwell, and by Him [Jesus Christ] to reconcile *all things* to Himself [God], by Him [Jesus Christ], whether things on earth or things in heaven, having made peace through the blood of His cross.

God has reconciled us to Himself through His Son Jesus Christ. This scripture also says that He reconciled *all things* to Himself through Christ Jesus. *All things*—all that Adam lost because of his disobedience has been brought back through the *cross* of Jesus Christ.

Jesus was made a curse that in return we might be redeemed from the curse and inherit the blessing of God.

Chapter Three

How long will a curse or blessing last?

When considering blessings and curses we must not miss one very important fact—once applied, both blessings and curses will continue until they are revoked! This means that there may be forces at work in our lives and families which were set in motion many years ago. Possibly we will have to deal with situations and circumstances which are determined not only by what has happened in our lifetime, but maybe by what happened many generations ago.

When God gave the Ten Commandments to Moses God said,

> For I, the Lord your God, am a jealous God, visiting the iniquity of the fathers on the children to the third and fourth generations of those who hate Me, but showing mercy to thousands, to those who

> love Me and keep My commandments (Ex 20: 5–6).

We can see that both blessings and curses continue throughout generations until they have been cancelled. I have no conviction that we can count to the third and fourth generation and then simply expect the curse, or for that matter the blessing, to just stop of its own accord. I believe the naming of the third and fourth generation is symbolic; it could be the sixth, seventh, or even one hundredth.

Here are a few examples for us to consider. The first is from the life of King David, at the time when Saul and his son Jonathan died. 2 Samuel 1:17, 21 reads:

> Then David lamented with this lamentation over Saul and over Jonathan his son.
>
> 'O mountains of Gilboa,
> let there be no dew,
> nor rain upon you,
> nor fields of offerings.
> For the shield of the mighty
> is cast away there!
> The shield of Saul,
> not anointed with oil.'

David proclaimed this approximately 3,000 years ago, of one particular group of mountains—Gilboa: 'Let there be no dew or rain.' Those of you who follow events in Israel today will know that the Jewish people have had remarkable success in replanting whole areas of their land, except one area. On the Gilboa heights they have not been able to make anything grow. Why? Because David pronounced a curse 3,000 years ago and that curse is still active today.

> Then Joshua charged them at that time, saying, 'Cursed be the man before the Lord who rises up and builds this city Jericho; he shall lay its foundation with his firstborn, and with his youngest he shall set up its gates (Josh 6:26).

This curse was pronounced after Israel had destroyed the city of Jericho. Almost 500 years later a man called Hiel of Bethel did the very thing which Joshua had pronounced the curse against. He rebuilt Jericho. 1 Kings 16:34 tells us:

> In his days [that is, the days of Ahab] Hiel of Bethel built Jericho. He laid its foundation with Abiram his firstborn, and with his youngest son Segub he set up its gates, according to the word of the Lord, which He had spoken through Joshua the son of Nun.

From the life of Jesus in the New Testament we have the story of the fig tree (Mk 11:14, 20–21). The only words Jesus spoke to it were, 'Let no one eat fruit from you ever again.' 'Now in the morning, as [the disciples] passed by, they saw the fig tree dried up from the roots. And Peter, remembering said [to Jesus], "Rabbi, look! The fig tree which You cursed has withered away." ' We need to realise that Jesus did not touch the tree, he just spoke words!

Words are powerful. The Scriptures tell us in Proverbs 18:21 that 'Death and life are in the power of the tongue'. So words, which are charged with power and pronounced as a blessing or a curse, can be the source of many circumstances in our lives. Words spoken, sometimes simply in jest, have become a curse because of the way they have been uttered, and the motivation behind them.

Just one example of the blessing of God continuing from generation to generation is found in the life of Abraham. Taking the story up at Genesis 22:15–18, God has requested that Abraham sacrifices his only son Isaac. Because of his willingness God says to him:

> ...in blessing I will bless you, and in multiplying I will multiply your descendants as the stars of the heaven and as the sand which is on the seashore; and your descendants shall possess the gate of their enemies. In your seed all the nations of the earth shall be blessed, because you have obeyed My voice.

This blessing was pronounced approximately 4,000 years ago and it is still at work today. All nations are blessed because of Abraham, whether natural or spiritual descendants, ie, those who have faith in the God of Abraham. 'If you are Christ's, then you are Abraham's seed, and heirs according to the promise' (Gal 3:29).

So we see that a curse will continue in time from generation to generation until revoked and annulled by the blood of Jesus Christ. There is no way to reverse a curse except through the cross of Jesus Christ. This means that the consequence of death, brought upon men and women through

Adam and Eve's sin, will continue in our lives until it is revoked and cancelled out. This in turn means that the consequences of that sin will also continue until revoked.

The price has been paid

The word 'redeemed' means, literally, to buy back. When someone sells an article to a pawnbroker, and then sometime later buys that article back, the word used is 'redeemed'. So when looking at Jesus Christ's work on the cross we need to see that He was purchasing back (redeeming) something that had been lost. In this book there is not the space to list all that Jesus bought back upon the cross for us, but only to mention a few of the blessings: Jesus took our sickness that we might have health; He took our poverty that we might be abundantly supplied; He took our sin in order that we might have life.

Redemption implies that something that was rightfully ours has been lost or stolen and we have now had it redeemed. Usually it also means that a price has had to be paid. Jesus has already paid the price for us upon the cross by shedding his blood so that we can have returned to us what Satan has taken from us.

What God intended to be rightfully ours has been stolen because of sin. All we have to do is to revoke the curse.

> Even so we, when we were children, were in bondage under the elements of the world. But when the

> fullness of the time had come, God send forth His Son, born of a woman, born under the law to redeem those who were under the law, that we might receive the adoption as sons. And because you are sons, God has sent forth the Spirit of His Son into your hearts, crying out, 'Abba Father!' Therefore you are no longer a slave but a son, and if a son, then an heir of God through Christ (Gal 4:3–7).

> Knowing that you were not redeemed with corruptible things...but with the precious blood of Christ (1 Pet 1:18–19).

> Being justified freely by His grace through the redemption that is in Christ Jesus (Rom 3:24).

Jesus has bought back for us all that Adam lost.

Some of you reading this book may not have found it easy to receive all that you feel God has to offer you. I would like to encourage you: although you may have found it difficult, we cannot say that the Word of God is wrong just because we have difficulty walking in the reality of it. We must never allow our experiences to annul the Word of God. God's Word is truth, and we must see anything we experience which is contrary to that Word as Satan's lie to deceive us. Your experience does not lessen the Word of God. Romans 3:4 says, 'Let God be true but every man a liar.'

We are able to receive all the promises of God by faith. Even when our physical conditions try to tell us something other than the Word of God says, we can still believe that by faith we are living in the blessings of God's Word. Confessing what the Word of God says will bring us into the reality of it.

Ecclesiastes 11:1 tells us to 'Cast your bread upon the waters, for you will find it after many days.' In the same way, when we cast the Word of God into our lives regularly, it will return to us.

Let us now go back to Genesis 3:16:

> I will greatly multiply your sorrow and your conception; in pain you shall bring forth children; your desire shall be for your husband, and he shall rule over you.

We can divide this into four parts for our consideration:

1 I will greatly multiply your sorrow and your conception
2 In pain you shall bring forth children
3 Your desire shall be to your husband
4 And he shall rule over you.

There are four definite parts to the verse, four individual subjects. Before we consider them I would like to state that it is not necessarily the case that all four subjects will be affecting your life. There may be one or two that you feel you can relate to in particular; some may feel that all four have somehow influenced their lives. The answer to all four aspects is the same.

Chapter Four

'I will greatly multiply your sorrow and your conception...'

Multiplication

All women, single or married, have, or should have a monthly menstruation. The word used in Scripture—sorrow—applies to our monthly menstruation. I feel there are many women who would readily describe their monthly menstruation as sorrow! Various factors determine the symptoms we each experience at this time of the month. First, I would like to establish the fact that there may well be some physical sensation at the outset of our seed being produced and starting its course, and ending in the rejection of the unfertilised egg, the first being in the middle of our cycle and the latter being our monthly menstruation. But in saying that, I want us to bear in mind our text which states quite clearly that there would be a multiplication of sorrow!

When I was at school I was taught my multiplication tables at an early age:

2 X 2 = 4
3 X 3 = 9

If you are going to multiply there has to be a basis from which to multiply. With the result of sin came the multiplication of the sensations which accompanied the cycle. This has resulted in many women experiencing depression, abnormal pain, water retention, irrational fears, and a whole number of other emotional stresses and tensions.

It can all be changed

God made our bodies to function and I do not believe any of the above symptoms (nor any other not mentioned) were in His plan. God, our Creator, is well able to keep our bodies in order. He made our hormones and had them finely balanced to produce all that was necessary to keep us healthy.

When considering the issue of menstruation we need to realise that through sin our bodies have been put out of balance; Satan has robbed us. We do not necessarily need deliverance from some evil, oppressive demon. We do not need healing for some part of our body that has been attacked by a disease, virus, or germ. All we need to do is to revoke the curse that has come because of sin. We need the result of death to be cancelled out in our lives.

One lady who came to me for prayer told how she had had demons cast out of her; she had received prayer for healing by all the evangelists and faith ministers who had visited her church, but she was still no better. Her husband was an elder of their church and his ministry was under stress because she was so debilitated by her monthly menstruation; it totally controlled their lives. She had been to medical specialists but was still living under the shadow of depression caused by hormone imbalance.

After sharing a thumbnail sketch of the principles stated I prayed with her and asked her to go home and share with her husband the things we had talked through, so, together, they should receive the freedom which the Lord Jesus Christ had provided for her life, revoking the consequences of death.

Eighteen months later I received a letter from her telling me that from that day she had been completely free. She had been able to live a normal life again, was involved with her husband's ministry and had no more trouble with depression, premenstrual tension and the excessive symptoms she had previously endured. Please note, all she did was to simply revoke the curse placed upon her by sin.

The truth is that we need to recognise the *full work* of the cross of Jesus Christ in every area of our lives. He did not do half a job on the cross. He completely restored us and brought within our reach God's highest for each and every one of us. He has taken us back to God's original plan, just as we saw in the previous chapter.

Involved in this area is freedom from the abnormalities of the menopause. Most doctors agree that the majority of problems during the menopause are caused by the hormones becoming unbalanced. Which hormone overpowers the other varies from person to person. The most common medical treatment is to try to bring the hormones into balance by some means or other, usually by controlled drugs. Hormone replacement therapy is another modern treatment.

God made our bodies and I feel He is the best One to keep them working perfectly. Even in the menopause we can have faith to apply the principles of the cross of Jesus Christ and know freedom to live victoriously. Here again we can revoke the curse caused by the consequences of sin.

Whoever—wherever!

These principles apply whoever we are and wherever we live.

A few years ago I had the privilege of visiting an African country with my husband, on one of his missionary crusades. I was asked by the local pastors who had invited us to speak to the women. After presenting the message which I felt God had given me for them, they asked me to teach some more. Here were people who were hungry for the Word of God. I had already been speaking for approximately one hour and they were wanting more!

I felt very clearly that the Holy Spirit was impressing upon me to share the same principles that I am sharing with you. Being in a foreign country and sensitive to their culture, I asked permission of the pastor to speak on this subject. Some of the local ministers had attended the ladies' meeting! (I never did find out if they were checking up on me or if it was just that they wanted to get as much from us as they could!) The pastor asked all the other men to leave. They went out of the door and sat along the side of the building. With no window frames or glass panes they could hear everything I said!

I took about half an hour. Immediately afterwards the men who could speak English came and thanked me, saying what a change this teaching was going to make in their churches. When I enquired what they meant I was promptly told that the women of their congregations were constantly making excuses for not attending church and teaching seminars. The main excuse was their monthly menstruation, the pain and other symptoms which they suffered. It is not just those of us in the Western world who suffer from the result of Eve's sin, but women everywhere!

Already I can hear some of you asking: 'What is normal?' 'What can I expect?' 'Is what I am experiencing the consequence of sin or is it as God intended?' 'Should I expect any change when I revoke the curse or is what I am already experiencing normal?'

Having listened to many women tell me about their experiences of menstruation, and having read relevant medical literature, I have come to the following conclusions. God's intention for us is that we should have a regular menstrual cycle, with no excessive pain; there should be no excessive discharge needing medical attention, and the length of our period should be between three and seven days. In addition to this I believe we should be able to live on an 'even keel' with no heights and depths of depression.

Chapter Five

'In pain you shall bring forth children...'

Natural birth was God's plan

Again the basic principle set out above applies. Because of sin, the pain involved in bearing children has been greatly multiplied. There is obviously some pain when one gives birth. The whole process of childbirth from conception involves a degree of pain. The changes brought about in a woman's body in order to produce a child are wonderful; it is therefore no great surprise that in the Psalms David exclaims, 'For I am fearfully and wonderfully made' (Ps 139:14). Many books written about the birth process give helpful information to the pregnant woman. My concern for the moment is with the pain level.

Contractions are necessary; some women

describe them as painful. The majority of women I have counselled have experienced some pain, but I feel that excessive, unbearable pain is a result of the curse brought about by sin.

Complications which I consider are also a consequence of Adam and Eve's sin often occur.

> And Adam was not deceived, but the woman being deceived, fell into transgression. Nevertheless she will be saved in childbearing if they continue in faith, love and holiness, with self-control (1 Tim 2:14–15).

These verses do not mean that we shall be saved from sin by giving birth to children. What they do mean is that we shall literally be saved from death when giving birth if as individuals we continue in faith, love, holiness and self-control. We can know wholeness, salvation and a total freedom from the abnormalities so often experienced in childbirth when we live godly lives.

With this scripture, as with so many others, there is a condition. We must live in holiness, continue in faith and love, with our lives under self-control. I feel this is important not only for our own well-being but also for the good of the child we are bearing. To seek to live on an even keel, in love with God, having faith that God will give us victory, and having self under control, will produce a baby that is easy to handle when it is born.

We can receive this freedom

At this point I would like to share with you my own testimony.

When I was carrying our son, Stephen (my first child), many people told me that I was so much like my mother. At that time, this was a very negative statement because she experienced excessive complications at the birth of both my brother and myself. The matron of the nursing home where my mother had been in confinement was a very close friend of our family and so knew the problems well. I have quite a small frame and those of you who know my husband (Don Double) will know that he is six foot five inches tall and has rather a large frame. All these negatives were screaming at me and I was becoming concerned, especially when my doctor told me that I might have twins, and if not, a very large baby!

At this time a friend of ours, a fellow minister, was visiting our church. Don and I had been looking closely at the scriptures concerning childbirth and had realised that it was God's intention that childbirth should be natural and free from tensions placed upon us by other people's experiences. We asked him to pray for me and claim what we had seen from Scripture. Stephen was born a month later and I can honestly say that I had a completely painless delivery. Although I was in labour for twenty-four hours I was able to watch Stephen being born. The delivery was in our own home. I slept through most of the first and second stages of labour, and I had no stitches even though he was eight pounds twelve ounces and twenty-two inches long! I give all the glory to God and the redemption purchased for me by Jesus Christ upon the cross.

Since then I have had two more children. Joel came into the world at nine pounds six ounces, Faith at eight pounds seven ounces. Both deliveries were again natural and painless. I would also like to add here that as a teenager I had experienced excessive pain during my monthly menstruation, but since claiming my rightful inheritance in Christ Jesus I have never 'suffered' any of the excesses I knew before.

I am not living in cloud-cuckoo-land (a fantasy land). I know that in the years to come I will go through the menopause but I am in faith, believing that what I have experienced over the years will again be made available to me, and I expect to go through my life knowing freedom from the result of Eve's sin! I have no reason to doubt that what has been a reality so far will remain a reality as I continue to seek to live in faith, love, holiness and self-control.

Our experiences versus the Word of God

Over the years I have talked to many Christian women who have challenged my belief, saying that this has not been their experience. I am persuaded that we do not annul the Word of God by our experience; we must seek to make the Word of God our experience.

If our lives do not tally with the Word of God it does not mean that the Word of God is wrong; it means that our experience is wrong. We must seek to change our experience to coincide with the Word of God.

For many of us, in addition to the consequences of sin which are common to women, there are curses of words which have been spoken. Sometimes well-meaning parents or teachers, trying to prepare us for womanhood, have made negative statements, about childbearing in particular. They have told us stories about other women's experiences in giving birth; or perhaps we have seen films which portray women screaming while giving birth. We may have read articles in women's magazines that have told of bad experiences in hospitals or doctors' surgeries; of babies that have been born in taxis, ambulances, cars, etc. because it has been impossible to reach the hospital in time. Stories also circulate about the menopause: women talk of hot flushes, bad pain, loss of memory and innumerable other symptoms. These stories sink into our minds and therefore we expect these things to happen because we have heard nothing else. Unbeknown to us these ideas have planted seeds in our subconscious which have become curses in our lives.

Throughout the past years I have often been asked to pray with young ladies who have a deep fear of bearing children. The fear has been so real that they have, as a result, not wished to be married. The only way to deal with these fears and bondages will be shared in the last chapter.

Chapter Six

'Your desire shall be to your husband...'

Battle of the sexes

Here is the basis for much of the bad feeling and attitudes between male and female that we experience in our society today.

Some of the consequences brought upon women because of sin have to do with a desire to be ruled and dominated by men, husbands in particular. To try to understand the full meaning of Genesis 3:16 we need to turn to the Hebrew word 'teshuqah', translated 'desire' in this verse. In researching this word I discovered that some Hebrew scholars have the following explanation: all Hebrew words are built on a stem, with a prefix, suffix or medial added, giving the basic stem a full range of meanings; by breaking it down into the Hebrew stem ‘shuq’, its prefix ‘te’, and then its ending ‘ah’, we come up with the sense of ‘to run repeatedly’, that is ‘to run back and forth’. To run back and forth necessitates a frequent turning around: running in one direction then turning to run in the opposite direction. So we could translate this phrase ‘You are continually turning towards your husband.’ There is the sense of turning away from God and running towards your husband, or, in the broader sense, turning away from God and running towards men.

This is especially noticeable among some single ladies, who appear to have an excessive desire to be married. Every man whom they meet is looked upon as a prospective husband.

In our ministry, Don and I have been involved with some Christian young ladies who have been affected in this way, and who have required ministry to be brought into freedom in this area. Often the obsession with getting married filled their whole lives. When a man befriended them they imagined they were as good as married, even before the second date. They were so obsessed with their desire to have a husband that they did not realise they were driving the young men away rather than attracting them. When the man became friendly with someone else and married her instead they became very depressed. They then felt rejected and more obsessed than ever!

One particular testimony comes to mind here. A middle-aged lady came to me for counselling; she had been divorced for some years and had had a number of ‘boyfriends’ since being divorced. She confessed to me that every day she would have thoughts such as 'I wonder if I'll meet *him* today.' Then when she did meet someone, 'I wonder if this is *him*?' She was overwhelmed constantly with thoughts of having a man in her life. In the end her life was ruled by these thoughts.

This kind of predicament is part of the curse which was placed upon women and which Satan has taken advantage of ever since. The Devil has taken advantage of us as women; consequently single women can get too caught up with the idea of married life being utopia that they become ineffective for God and His kingdom. Let me tell you now that married life is not utopia—nor the answer to life and all its problems. Marriage is hard work! You have to work at marriage all your life to make it a success. If you are not prepared for some hard labour don't get married! The effort does not end when we take our marriage vows, it starts with our marriage vows!

We need to see that this illusion we have been under is a result of the consequences of sin, and needs to be reversed and revoked. No demon need necessarily be cast out, no healing of the memory, no emotional healing. (Because of their obsession some women may subsequently need ministry in these areas but it is not usually the root of the matter.)

Single or married—is there a difference?

I can remember two young ladies in particular who were in their mid-twenties and feeling very much left on the shelf. It was obvious that they considered themselves second-class citizens because they were not married. They were prayed for, and the curse was revoked. Within a year they had both become engaged and were subsequently married, simply because they were free from the uncontrollable desire to be married and have a man rule over them.

The main root is the result of sin entering the world. Even after the marriage some women seem to have an unnatural desire to be dominated by their husbands. I have met some women who seem to fall apart whenever their husbands are away, unable to cope with their children, housework, careers or their own lives. They have become dependent upon their husbands for everything. I believe the Scripture has some clear teaching on a wife's submission to her husband, but there is also just as much in Scripture about a woman having a fulfilled life, complementing her husband, working alongside him and becoming a very worthy part of the marriage.

The point we are looking at is evident not only in married women but can also affect single ones too. Satan will take every opportunity to bring us into bondage. This is typical of the way he has twisted the consequences of the curse of death brought upon Eve; he has adversely affected the lives of women of all ages.

There is one scripture which I feel puts the difference between single and married women's lives very aptly:

> There is a difference between a wife and a virgin. The unmarried woman cares about the things of the Lord, that she may be holy both in body and in spirit. But she who is married cares about the things of the world—how she may please her husband (1 Cor 7:34).

This scripture is particularly relevant to me personally. My husband is away on average 60 per cent of every year. There are times when I feel like a single person (or at least a single-parent family!), and am able to care about the things of the Lord so much more easily than when my husband is at home. When he is home my concern is very much turned to 'the things of the world, and how I may please my husband'. I can relate to the literal Hebrew meaning of turning away from God and running to my husband.

For the single woman there is the positive side of caring about the things of the Lord. 'Seek ye the kingdom of God; and all these things shall be added unto you' (Lk 12:31, AV). To find what 'all these things' are we need to look to some of the earlier verses in Luke chapter 12. Verse 22 instructs us not to worry about what we shall eat, nor about what we are to wear. Verse 30 tells us that our Father knows that we need these things. Verses 27 and 28 tells us that the lilies in the field are better clothed than Solomon was. God knows how to look after the grass of the field so how much more will he clothe us, 'O you of little faith'! Knowing that God is not only capable of looking after us but also wants to look after us puts a different slant on our relationship with Him. Turning towards God rather than turning away from Him draws Him even closer.

What about submission?

Until sin came into the world there appears to be no reference in Scripture to Adam having to be told by God that he was the head of Eve. We have no record of Eve being told that she had to submit to Adam. Up to that point there had been no thought of one being better, or superior to the other. Adam did not 'lord it' over Eve.

The Word of God says in Ephesians 5:22, 'Wives submit to your own husbands, as to the Lord', but it does not mean that we are to be doormats, inferior, or any less persons in our own right. God created us all with brains to enable us to think, have our own opinions and ideas and to be creative.

Submission is an attitude not just an action. Whatever our surroundings and circumstances may be, we can have an attitude of submission, believing God that His will will be done in our lives because we are being obedient to His Word. Note that the Scripture says we should submit to our own husband *as to the Lord.*

One day my husband and I found ourselves counselling a lady who felt she had a deep problem. Her husband, who did not share her commitment to Christ, was a retired, successful, professional man. She had a desire to go back to work and her husband agreed. Two opportunities were open to her—one in a local business where she would receive a fair wage, the other in a Christian school to do voluntary work. She felt strongly that God was directing her to the Christian school, but thought her husband would not approve, thus taking her out of God's will. We gave her counsel that she should go home and submit to her husband. Her first reaction was that this would be so strange to them both as she had always led her own life.

She duly went home, told her husband that she had spoken to us and related to him exactly what we had said to her about submitting to him. His reaction was that this would alter their relationship considerably. She was thrilled when her husband told her to take the voluntary job. She had been obedient to God's Word, and trusted that He would work out the details for her.

The Bible says that if we cannot love our brother whom we can see how can we love God whom we cannot see (1 Jn 4:20). In the same way, if we cannot submit our will to that of our husband, whom we can see, how can we learn to submit our lives to God, whom we cannot see.

Am I inferior?

God made Eve to complement Adam, not to be inferior to him. The fact that Eve was created after Adam does not mean that she was inferior or made any less in the image of God.

Genesis 1:27 says, 'In the image of God He created him; male and female He created them.' Both male and female have been created in the image of God.

1 Corinthians 15:46–47 tells us, 'However, the spiritual is not first, but the natural, and afterward the spiritual. The first man was of the earth, made of dust; the second Man is the Lord from heaven.' Our natural life came first, then our spiritual, when we were born again by the Spirit of God. I am sure none of us would say that our spiritual life is inferior to our natural life, rather the opposite. So why do we suppose that because women were made second they *must* be inferior? How can anything which is made in the image of God ever be inferior, no matter when it was made? Just as our spiritual life would have no expression if we had no natural life—one without the other is not enough—so with male and female—one without the other does not fully express God's plan. Neither is superior nor inferior to the other but each complements the other.

It was only as a consequence of the curse of death that Adam felt superior and had a need to dominate Eve. Before this they had been given dominion only over creation.

Chapter Seven

'And he [your husband] shall rule over you.'

Who is the leader?

Adam and Eve appear to have had clearly defined roles. Because of what God said abut the consequences of the curse in their lives we can assume that Adam was to be the provider. In Genesis 3:17–19 God said that the ground would be cursed and that Adam would toil all the days of his life, because thorns and thistles would grow with the seed which Adam planted. Therefore, to be able to produce food for his family, he would have to work hard.

The result of the curse upon Eve would be that she would reproduce in pain and that her relationship to her husband would also be affected (Gen 3:16). Eve was to be, as the Amplified Version of the

Bible puts it, a helper meet (suitable, adapted, completing) for him.

Eve allowed the serpent to trick her into eating of the forbidden fruit. I feel the main issue was that she stepped outside the role God had given her and took it upon herself to do a job God had given to her husband—to harvest the fruit of the field for their sustenance.

Adam rebelled against God. In fact he put the blame upon God by saying, 'The woman whom You gave to be with me...' (Gen 3:12). In other words, 'I would not have eaten of the fruit if she had not given it to me. It was all your fault, God, for making her.' But he stood before God on his own and had to answer to God for his own action and non-action, just as Eve had to answer to God for herself. Eve owned her sin and said the serpent had tempted her. Adam sinned in not taking responsibility for his own actions, or non-actions. Some husbands retreat into themselves and become inactive, and even acquiescent. This in turn causes their wives many problems because the husbands opt out from their God-given leadership and responsibilities.

It was not part of Adam's nature to dominate his wife. He had been given dominion only over the creatures, not over his wife! From then on, as a result of Eve's folly, Adam lorded it over and dominated her.

This again was multiplied—it became excessive. Ever since, womankind has been fighting to gain an equal position. Some men have been so provoked by this that they have, or feel, a need to have control over women, always wanting to dominate and lord it over their wives, daughters, fellow women workers, and so on. There seems to be a need in their lives to rule over someone, especially a woman.

If I don't fight I'll lose!

In the account of creation in Genesis man was given only one part to control and dominate—the animals and vegetation. Because men have allowed control to come into their relationship with women, women have developed an aggressive attitude towards men and constantly fight to regain their rightful place.

Throughout history women in every generation have fought in some way for equality with men. The Women's Liberation Organisation (which, incidentally, had its official commencement in eighteenth century, so is not quite such a modern-day organisation as many seem to think), feminist movements, Equal Rights for Women and other similar organisations, have developed out of a similar motivation. They are trying to bring freedom into many areas of life for women, but are doing it with wrong motives and attitudes and not dealing with the root issue. Unfortunately, this aggression has been brought into the church, and today many Christian women are fighting within the church of Jesus Christ from a worldly standpoint, instead of dealing with the real issue—sin—and the result of Adam and Eve's sin.

We do not need to fight for what is already ours

by right. The battle is over; Jesus was victorious over death and hell on the cross. Jesus has redeemed us and all we need to do is live in the good of what He purchased for us upon the cross. It is important for us to get our attitudes and motivations right and to leave the other to God.

Freedom from the result of Eve's sin is ours by right as children of God; neither Satan nor any man has any right to rob us. It will become part of our lives as our relationship with God is right. God desires us to live in victory, and therefore has made provision for us to live as He created us to live, being what He fashioned us to be—a helper, meet, suitable, adaptable, and completing our husbands. We can enlarge on this concept, I believe. Women in general, I feel, have been created to complete men, in general, whoever they are—fathers, husbands, brothers, church leaders, fellow workers, friends, and so on.

Let us face facts. Men would not be here today if it were not for women, and women would not be here today if it were not for men! Together, as man and woman, completing each other, we can fulfil God's plan. The church would be incomplete without a balance of men and women; together we bring God glory. We need to see the concept of male and female together, each fulfilling the role which God has made for us, and finding satisfaction in that role.

When God created Eve out of Adam's side He had a plan in mind. Among all the created beings which God had already made Adam had not found himself a mate. Therefore, God had to make a special creation just to meet Adam's need of a companion. So in fashioning Eve He must have had a special blueprint. There were certain things that had to be built into her. She had to be perfect, not only to fit God's plan, but Adam's needs. We were created in the image of God to fit man. How wonderful! I was created to do something special! That special job was to be a complement to man! Therefore, I was created with extra, special abilities! One of those abilities was adaptability. Another was to be a helper. Just as Jesus said He would go away and send another Helper, so we were sent as a helper to man. What a privilege! I am not just an afterthought. I was made with extra special thought in God's mind, planned before creation began!

God's order

In 1 Corinthians 11:3 Paul says, 'But I want you to know that the head of every man is Christ, the head of woman is man, and the head of Christ is God.' Contained in this one verse is God's divine order for us. God, Christ, man, woman. Once we have been born again by the Spirit of God and been redeemed by the blood of Jesus Christ we have become part of the kingdom of God. We are then living in the realm where Jesus Christ is Lord and we come into a new order, God's order. In this new order our past achievements, our standing in society, our position, counts as nothing in God's sight.

When we can believe this then we will be able to live positively and in victory; it will mean that, mentally, we are no longer under anyone's control, only God's by the power of His Holy Spirit.

Yes, even when we feel emotionally on edge God can give us the victory. Our emotions play a vital role in our lives as women; they dictate so often the way we behave and what we feel. Our emotions can vary according to our monthly cycle. We need to become aware of what is happening to our own bodies and trust God to keep us in victory.

The key is to appropriate what Jesus did for us on the cross and claim our freedom from emotional stresses.

Understand yourself

Some of the most common flaws in a woman's character stem from the fact that she does not understand her own body and what is going on inside her. Our emotions are being attacked as a result of the curse brought upon Adam and Eve so that the Devil can gain an advantage.

Our emotions are very much controlled by how well our ovaries function. There can be various reasons for hormone imbalance. One of the most common and major contributors to imbalance is that our ovaries are not producing the correct balance of hormones. When this happens we soon find ourselves experiencing heights and depths of emotion. This is particularly noticeable during the menopause. When our ovaries are not working properly we often find ourselves in tears. Anything, no matter how small, can suddenly tip the balance and we find ourselves in floods of tears! We don't understand why and are unable to explain to those around what has happened.

Recognising what is happening to our emotions can be one of the most releasing discoveries of our lives. The challenge of how to cope with the situation comes when we realise what is happening.

God has not left us to get on with our lives and work things out for ourselves. He has given us His Holy Spirit to help us. In Galatians 5:22–23 we see one of the most practical workings of the Holy Spirit in our lives:

> But the fruit of the Spirit is love, joy, peace, long-suffering, kindness, goodness, faithfulness, gentleness, self-control. Against such there is no law.

One of the fruits of the Holy Spirit mentioned here is self-control. Self under control! As long as we live on this earth we will have emotions, because that is the way God has made us. In our own strength it would be hard graft to control our emotions, but with the Holy Spirit to help us we have the potential to keep our emotions under control.

When our ovaries do not function properly our hormones become imbalanced and our emotions run wild. The answer is faith in God, believing Him to keep our whole being in balance, looking to the Holy Spirit to aid us and give us His fruit of self-control. Believing that the redemption purchased for us upon the cross of Jesus Christ is sufficient brings us healing in our emotions.

There are some women whose emotions have been repeatedly damaged and hurt. The wounds are often very deep, but these women need healing from their hurts in order that they can begin to believe God to bring them into freedom in their monthly menstruation.

What we *feel* plays a major part in most people's lives. As women we often find ourselves grappling with emotions and feelings that we somehow find it difficult to believe God can help us with. We receive our healing, and anything else we need, from God, by faith and not by our feelings. In Mark 11:24 Jesus says, 'Therefore I say to you, whatever things you ask when you pray, believe that you receive them, and you will have them.' We receive healing when we pray, not when we *feel* better. Our faith must stand upon the Word of God and not on what we feel.

We sometimes have difficulty in receiving healing because we do not accept the authority of the Word of God. When we can positively confess with faith what God's Word says then our faith is living, and there will be a manifestation of that which God has already committed Himself to in His Word.

Chapter Eight

Following the last two points discussed there are other issues which I would like to address.

Do words which are spoken affect us?

Many young women have been brought under a curse by words spoken by others abut marriage. The divorce rate has also added to their fears that their marriage will not last and that they will be rejected and left stranded by their husbands. Words such as: 'It won't work!' 'Men only want us for our bodies!' 'There is nothing in the sexual experience for women.' 'Be careful or he'll walk over you and you will become a doormat!' 'What makes you suppose that you're any different from anyone else and think that you have a special relationship!'

The list could go on and on of negative statements made to women which have infiltrated their minds and become a curse. Divorces have taken place, marriages have been broken up, people have been rejected, women have ended up in a marriage relationship where they are unsatisfied sexually. The good news is that we don't have to live under these threats any more. There is freedom, there is release! It is not a complicated, long, drawn out deliverance process—it can happen the moment we can recognise the root, and deal with it as God's Word says we must.

At the close of one of our meetings a middle-aged lady came forward for prayer. She had been brought into the meeting in a wheelchair, but was able to walk a little with the aid of a pair of crutches. As my husband was about to pray for her, he felt that he was going to be just another in a long line of ministers who had prayed for her without success. Quietly he prayed, asking the Lord to give him the key to her problem. Using the gift of the word of knowledge by the Holy Spirit he felt there was a curse operating in her life. Rather falteringly he asked her if the word 'curse' meant anything to her. Immediately she replied, 'Why, yes. My father cursed me the day I was born!' When her mother was expecting her, both her parents desired a male child. At delivery, when it was revealed that the baby was a girl, her father duly pronounced a curse upon her life. She could never remember a day when she was without some physical problem. As she had grown older the problems had become worse. Now, in middle age, she was confined to walking with crutches and using a wheelchair to get around, totally relying upon others. My husband

and his colleague prayed for her and revoked the curse upon her life.

The next morning she came to the meeting in a taxi, unaided, without wheelchair or crutches. During the worship time we saw her dancing and praising God. She was even wearing a normal pair of shoes, something which she had been unable to do for at least ten years. She had been totally freed from the curse which had plagued her life for so long.

Doctors' surgeries are full of women who don't really have anything medically wrong with them—the problems are of a spiritual nature. The hurts go deep into the subconscious where medical aids and doctors' prescriptions cannot reach. Words spoken are so very powerful. If only we would believe it we would change not only our own lives, but help to change the lives of those around us, because our words would no longer bring curses upon them.

Female or male?

Another problem many women face which I consider a direct result of the curse upon us is the whole aspect of our femininity. In our generation today there are women who appear to be manly in character. (Obviously I can only speak of this present generation, although I feel sure it has been true of every generation from Adam and Eve.)

I believe God created all women with the ability to be feminine. You may rightly ask—but how do we know what is femininity as God created it? My only answer is that there is a certain beauty in the feminine character which appears in all women in any age or culture. As I have had the privilege to travel in ministry over the years, in whatever country or culture I have visited I have noticed that the women of the nation have a beauty not manifested in the men. Although their colour and the mode of dress may be vastly different, there seems to be a distinguishing mark of beauty in the female form which is undeniable.

One of these characteristics is seen very clearly in family life. When a youngster falls and hurts himself or herself who do they run to first of all? In most cases their mother. There seems to be a comforting spirit about a mother, placed by God in her, that responds to a child with a hurting knee, hand or head; it brings a special solace. In saying this I do not mean that men have been left out. There are certainly some men who are as comforting as women, but in general females appear to have an ability to comfort.

In John 14:16 Jesus tells his disciples that He is going to send them another 'Comforter'. I am convinced that Jesus chose His words carefully to explain who the Holy Spirit was. 'Comforter' is a real explanation of the Holy Spirit's work in our lives. The Holy Spirit is a part of the Godhead, and therefore His character is part of God. When God created Adam and Eve he imparted to them all of His own characteristics, one of which was comfort. I feel that this aspect of God's character was placed mainly in women. There are other characteristics of God which have generally been placed in women, and others which have been placed mainly in men.

Another characteristic which we find predominates in woman is that of being a homemaker. Again, I have observed as I have travelled that it does not matter what the home is—mud hut, chalet, flat, bedsitter, house or palace—there seems to be a gift of 'nest making' in women. Wherever we find a home with a woman in it, whether it is found in the inner city, the country or even the African bush, there is the evidence of the gift of making a *home*.

I can remember that on one occasion, when my husband and I were invited to speak at a church, we were accommodated by a kind single gentleman. As soon as I entered the home I could tell that no woman had had a hand in it; it was a bachelor's home! Somehow there is a difference! That is not to say that men cannot make a home, but a woman in the home appears to make a lot of difference, not only to the decor but also to the atmosphere.

If only I'd been born a man!

There are women in our generation who have been so misused by men, and influenced by words, that they have taken on male characteristics. They make statements such as, 'I'd rather be a man!' 'Why did God make me a woman?' 'If God had made me a man then I would have been able to do this job!' 'If only I'd been a boy I could have achieved my ambition, but because I am a woman I am living in a condemned state, relegated to certain jobs with no career prospects!'

As they say these things they curse themselves

and are unable to break free from the moulds they have made for themselves. On the other hand there are women who, because they have cursed themselves with negative thoughts about being a woman, have begun to act in a manly way. They have taken on themselves the characteristics of a man in order to accomplish their goals. Because they are then unable to distinguish between the feminity which God has placed in them, and the manliness which they have taken upon themselves, they become overpowered by their soulish desire to be like a man. They become dominant, over authoritative, bossy, and excessively pushy. They are unable to be feminine, and are taken over by a spirit which appears to control their lives, always taking the lead and desiring to be in control and the head of everything in which they are involved.

In my own life I know that without God I could have easily become like this. I only have one brother, but I also have a male cousin who spent a great deal of time with my brother and me. As we were growing up, the three of us did a lot together and I quickly developed into a tomboy. I liked to try to do all that my two male counterparts could do! What saved me was the fact that I have a wonderful mother who taught me to do all the feminine things as well. She did not push me aside and say that she could do jobs quicker than I could. She gave me room to make mistakes with the cooking, dressmaking, ironing, etc. I grew up able to look after the home, but also knowing how to climb trees, do small repairs to my bicycle, know how the engine of a car works and able to hit a target when shooting a gun!

I am convinced that the problems of manliness in women are a direct result of the curse which we have been considering.

The Devil is out to confuse us in whatever way he can in our roles as men and women. This is an area which he has targeted and today we are reaping the harvest!

When I was in my teens I had to travel to school by a service bus. During the course of the journey the bus would stop and on to it would step a man—well, we all thought he was a man. He would dress quite smartly with a three-piece suit, collar and tie. But we could never make out why his voice was so feminine.

One day I spoke to my mother about him. I was very lovingly told that he was not a man, but a woman who liked to dress as a man! Later, when I fully understood, I realised that the woman and her partner were living in a lesbian relationship. This is an extreme, but nevertheless it illustrates to what extent the Devil has twisted people and confused their minds and lives.

Let us not be ignorant of his devices (2 Cor 2:11) but ensure that our lives as Christian women are portraying the characteristics of femininity which God has given to us.

Girls today have to stand up for their rights in schools and colleges; many of them have become manly without realising what is happening. The effects are obvious in some, more subtle in others. I have had to help more than one young lady to understand that to constantly wear trousers and masculine attire is not expressing the character which God has placed within her.

God has created us as, some would put it, the 'fairer sex'. Let's stay that way. I don't mean the 'dumb blonde' image, but I do mean the feminine woman image.

Chapter Nine

Housewife merely?

Proverbs 31:10–31 gives a very clear picture of the virtuous wife. Taking this as an example, we can clearly see the characteristics of a woman. If we tried to follow this we would soon find our lives very, very full. We have to be not only a wife and mother who cares and tends to the needs of her family, but also a career woman with a good business sense.

In verse 11 we see someone in whom her family trusts and finds deep security; so much so that in verse 28, not only do her children honour her but her husband also praises her.

Verse 12 shows she has a total commitment to her husband and their relationship.

In verse 16 we find a person who is seizing every opportunity to better herself and her family.

Verse 19 tells us that she not only cares generally

for her family, she even makes the materials for their clothing!

She also makes time for others less fortunate than herself and her family (v 20).

Then verses 25 and 26 indicate she is a person who has a spiritual walk with God that can sustain not only herself, but also her family.

It is quite a daunting task to fulfil these requirements without looking any further into the other verses.

I have known some women who have read this passage and been completely bowled over by it. But every scripture is given for us to profit by, and this one in particular is one which we must take to heart and seriously consider.

Or career girl?

In no way do I want you to feel that I am saying we cannot hold down good jobs as women. Our generation needs Christians who are at the top of their professions. We need to be the best we can for God with the gifts which He has given us.

In Acts chapter 16 we read about Lydia. I am told by many scholarly students of the Bible that Lydia was a professional woman. In Bible times a seller of purple would have been producing the most expensive cloth of the day. Most probably she was not only selling it, but producing it, employing divers who obtained the sea urchin from which the dye was made. In other words, we see a woman at the top of her profession and she was a Christian! Let's take her as an example and be successful too.

Going back to our passage in Proverbs 31:10–31, let us look at some verses in the light of being a career woman.

Verse 14 shows that the complexities of the catering trade and knowing where the best produce is to be purchased is also within the grasp of the ideal wife!

Verse 16 impresses on me how much the ideal wife must have known about the business world, especially land prices, and the quality of the soil, in order to produce the vines. I have met many women today who would know nothing about buying land, planting vines (or the equivalent in our day). Yet here the Bible is telling us that an ideal wife should know about such things!

In verse 24 we are told that the ideal wife can also compete in the business and commercial world.

Don't be overawed by these biblical women. Instead, let them challenge us not to sit at home and vegetate, but rise up and obtain important information on how we can succeed out in the 'High Street'.

How important are role models?

Young people are influenced by their own peers as well as by the example set them at home. Parents help to shape their children's characters. No matter how often you may say, 'Don't do as I do, but do as I say,' you will quickly discover that what you are is of more importance than what you say to your children.

If we are to produce adults of the future who will

count in life, I feel as parents we must watch very carefully what we are reproducing in our present young generation.

How Dad treats his wife will be taken up by his offspring. How Mum relates to her husband will be closely noticed by her own children. The way you run your home and how you as husband and wife develop your roles will be applied by your children to their future marriage relationships, presuming of course that they marry, but herein lies another problem. Some young people, because of the friction in their home, vow never to marry, or never to have a home like the one they have so far experienced. Some even run away from home as soon as they can because they cannot cope with the tensions and pressures between their parents.

These problems again stem from the same root as all the others we have looked at, ie, Satan's desire to frustrate the purposes of God for His creation. But once again there is an answer for those who have found Jesus Christ as Lord and Saviour. We do not have to live under the consequences of the curse of death.

And what about competitiveness?

In today's society we see women entering into activities which in the past have always been considered a man's domain. We have women's football teams, women's cricket teams, even women body builders, women's anything teams so it seems! It appears that women are saying, 'Anything a man can do I (we) can do better!'

A spirit of competitiveness has arisen and been bred into us. Not just man against woman, but child against child, brother against sister, student against student. Wherever we turn there is this competitive spirit. In the home, in the school, in the college, on the sports field, in the office, in the factory, in the bedroom even, there seems to be someone vying for the top place, needing to have the upper hand; someone wanting the power and authority, trying to take the lead.

The first sin ever committed was Satan's attempt to be equal with God (Is 14:12–13; Ezek 28:1–19). Satan was the first one to be competitive—to have the desire to be as good as, if not better than, another. Adam and Eve were already made in the image of God but Satan tempted them to become *equal* with God!

> For God knows that in the day you eat of it [that was the tree of the knowledge of good and evil] your eyes will be opened, and you will be like God, knowing good and evil (Gen 3:5).

Jesus had the same problem among his disciples according to Mark 10:35–45. But what was Jesus' conclusion?

> You know that those who are considered rulers over the Gentiles lord it over them, and their great ones exercise authority over them. Yet it shall not be so among you; but whoever desires to become great among you shall be your servant. And whoever of you desires to be first shall be slave of all. For even the Son of Man did not come to be

served, but to serve, and to give His life a ransom for many (Mk 10:42–45).

Attitudes count

1 Corinthians chapter 9 portrays one who goes into strict training: Paul says that he disciplines and brings his own body into subjection; *his own body*, not pitting himself aggressively *against* someone else, in order to prove himself better than another. He used strict training principles for his own body. Then in 2 Timothy 2:5 Paul tells us, 'If anyone competes in athletics, he is not crowned unless he competes according to the rules.'

There are right attitudes to have towards others. One of these is shown us in 2 Corinthians: 'We... will not boast beyond our proper limits, but will confine our boasting to the field God has assigned to us' (2 Cor 10:13, NIV). As women we must not be in competition against our menfolk because God has given us different roles which will complement those of men.

Many of us feel we need to compete because we lack confidence in ourselves. Therefore, we are always trying to prove not only to ourselves, but also to others, that we are either equal or better than them. This is regularly seen among girls and boys at school, in the playground and in the home. We do not have to compete for a position which God has already given us!

We can be secure and confident when we have placed ourselves under God's order for our lives and seek to be the best for Him in that position.

Next time you find yourself in the middle of a heated argument which is getting rather bitter, try to stop and consider what is behind the problem. More often than not you will discover it is a competitive spirit; one person trying to be better than the other, both feeling they are right and the other wrong. It is the same if it is between brother and sister, husband and wife, parent and child or fellow workers. Understand that we are in a spiritual battle; we are not wrestling against other humans, but against principalities, powers and rulers of spiritual forces (Eph 6:12).

Feeling inadequate?

You have probably read this far and begin to feel that it is all too far out of reach. The goal is too high, the ideal beyond the realm of possibility. But wait a moment . . . is God a bad architect? When He created you it was in His own image. Do you think He left a part of Himself behind? Luke 14:28–30 records Jesus asking if a man, intending to build a tower, will not first sit down and count the cost to see if he has enough to finish it. God would have done just that for us. He sat down and so designed us that we have the ability to do the job *he* planned for us. Each one of us has the potential to be the person God wants us to be. We have the capabilities, especially when we know Christ's power in our lives. Through His redemption we are adequate. We need to appropriate His redemption.

Chapter Ten

Blessings or curses?

Now, I want us to look at Deuteronomy 28:1–14. Contained in these verses are the blessings of God which will be ours as we obey the voice of God.

I firmly believe that these blessings were what God intended for Adam and Eve if they had continued to obey God's voice and had not been disobedient. If we, in Christ, have reclaimed all that Adam lost, we must also believe that all these blessings are ours, too, when we enter into redemption and are obedient to God.

In the context of our subject let us look at verse 4: 'Blessed shall be the fruit of your body…, and then verse 11: 'The Lord will grant you plenty of goods, in the fruit of your body…'. God is promising us that He will bring His blessing upon the fruit of our bodies, ie, children, when we obey His voice. If God's blessing is to be on the fruit of our womb then

I feel we can believe God for natural childbirth with no complications. As part of God's gift of grace to us we can experience this blessing as our inheritance.

In Exodus 1:19 we have the testimony of the midwives, who said that the Hebrew women were not like the Egyptian women. Their babies were born quickly before the midwives could get to them. I am aware of the thought that the midwives were deceitful and probably telling Pharaoh lies. In verse 21 of the same chapter we are told, '...because the midwives feared God....' Knowing just a little about Jewish culture, I am sure that a Hebrew midwife who feared God would not tell downright lies! So I feel the testimony of the midwives stands, even if they did use it as an excuse to Pharaoh. I therefore see no reason to believe that this should not also be our testimony as heirs of God's grace; that as Christian women we can believe God to keep us healthy and well during pregnancy so that we have natural, quick deliveries of our children. Living with the blessing of God upon our life is the normal Christian life.

There seems to be only one condition in Scripture which God requires of us, and that is obedience to Him. Obedience will bring His blessing and disobedience will bring a curse and all its consequences into our lives. The rest of Deuteronomy chapter 28 consists entirely of curses which will be our portion if we are disobedient to God's voice and Word.

What about my relationship to God?

This brings us to the point of our personal relationship with God. We can only expect the blessing of God upon our lives when we obey Him, and one of the very first things which we need to do is to repent of our sin.

Jesus tells us, 'Unless you repent you will all likewise perish' (Lk 13:3, 5). And in Romans we find, 'The wages of sin is death, but the gift of God is eternal life in Christ Jesus our Lord' (Rom 6:23). The curse of death was the wage paid for sin from Adam and Eve onward, but God has given us the gift of eternal life through the death of His Son upon the cross.

If you wish to receive the gift of eternal life there is only one way, and that is through the Lord Jesus Christ. This involves accepting Him as God's only begotten Son and believing that no one can come to God the Father except through Him (Jn 14:6).

Repentance of our own personal sin is the very first step of obedience which we need to take. We must believe that Jesus Christ died upon the cross, and shed His blood to cleanse us from our sin, bringing us back to God. Then, when we ask Him to come and take over our lives as Saviour and make Him our Lord, we will receive His forgiveness and salvation from the consequences of sin.

We cannot lean upon anyone else. God requires us, as individuals, to have a relationship with Him. God has no grandchildren; He only has sons. We cannot say as Adam did, 'The woman (or in our case the man) you gave me, is the reason why I cannot have a relationship with you.' No one—

father, husband, mother, brother, sister, church leader or church member—is responsible for our relationship with God as Father.

Over the years that we have been in ministry, my husband and I have learnt, through counselling, that there are many people who cannot relate to God as Father. There can be many reasons why this is so, but mostly they relate to a person's experience with their own earthly father. It could be that their father has abused their mother, and perhaps them as well, using domination and often violence, even sexual abuse. Therefore, when they try to relate to God as their heavenly Father, all they can see is the memory of their earthly father.

The problem is not always a memory of violence or abuse. It could be simply caused by a father who left them; a father who was never available to them; a father who did not give them any true love and affection but who was distant and unapproachable; a father who was always there to wallop them, disciplining them or correcting them, but never to enjoy their presence and have fun with them; a father who never took responsibility for them, leaving it all to his wife.

There are also people who never knew who their fathers were. They were brought up by their mothers as single-parent families. This has resulted in them having an orphan spirit. They do not know how to relate to God as Father because they have never had a father with whom to relate. On occasions, we have met people born out of wedlock, who have asked for help because they felt 'fatherless', even though in some cases their parents married after their birth.

There appears to be an endless list of reasons why people are unable to relate to their fathers. In Jesus Christ we can be freed from all the reasons there have ever been, or ever will be, and have the ability to enter into a real father–child relationship with God, our heavenly Father.

We stand with, or fall from God on our own. We must take responsibility for ourselves. We need to develop our own faith in God so that we can see in the Scriptures what God requires of us as women.

In turn this will mean that we can hear God's voice clearly, for ourselves, and can claim from Scripture our role in life as it should be, working it out day by day. God does not require that we just hear Him via others, He desires to talk with us individually as His own children. He has things to say to us personally, as our Father, by the Holy Spirit.

If we wish to distinguish between our Father God speaking to us, or some other voice, then we need to take heed of the teaching of Jesus Christ in John chapter 10. We must train ourselves to know His voice. Jesus uses the picture language of a shepherd and his sheep to teach us. In verses 3 and 5 he tells us, '...and the sheep hear his voice; and he calls his own sheep by name and leads them out.... Yet they will by no means follow a stranger, but will flee from him, for they do not know the voice of strangers.'

Some years ago, we first got our dog 'Honey'. Our children, being normal children, used always to be calling her. She became so accustomed to this continual calling that in the end she hardly ever went to them when they called. I called her by whistling, and every time I did so she would come directly to me. She knew my whistle. When we took her out with other dogs their owners would whistle too, but our dog would not respond. This taught me clearly how we should become so sensitive to our Master's voice that we will respond instantly.

There are so many voices crying out in the world but we must train our heart to hear our Shepherd's voice. Then we will be able to be obedient and walk in the blessing which God has prepared for us who love Him.

> But it is written: 'Eye has not seen, nor ear heard, nor have entered into the heart of man the things which God has prepared for those who love Him.' But God has revealed them to us through His Spirit. For the Spirit searches all things, yes, the deep things of God (1 Cor 2:9–10).

Chapter Eleven

Receiving freedom

In this final chapter it is my desire to give you some practical help to bring you into freedom and liberty from curses that have been brought into your life by your ancestors' sin (Adam and Eve's), or by words which you have heard or read. No matter through whom or how the bondage came, I believe it is God's will for you to be free.

The *New International Version of the Bible* translates Galatians 5:1 thus: 'It is for *freedom* that Christ has set us free! Stand firm, then, and do not let yourselves be burdened again by a yoke of slavery' (emphasis added).

Again, in John 8:36: 'If the Son shall set you free you shall be free indeed.'

2 Corinthians 3:17 tells us, 'Where the spirit of the Lord is there is liberty.'

King David, in Psalm 119:45 says, 'I will walk

about in *freedom* for I have sought out your precepts' (emphasis added).

Bondage is undesirable to any person. For hundreds of years our ancestors have fought and been martyred for the sake of freedom. People have fought against being dominated by another person, or group of people. Nations have fought so as not to be ruled by another nation. My own nation of Britain fought only fifty years ago, many fellow countrymen giving their lives in order that today we could be free to rule ourselves and not come under another country's domination.

Most of us love our freedom, and as human beings will fight to maintain that freedom. Yet we women in the Christian community have sat back silently, living our lives in complete bondage. Now is the time for us to truly enter into the freedom which Jesus Christ our Lord and Saviour died to give us.

The first step into this freedom is to acknowledge that we are in bondage, and to name freely the area in which we want to be free. I mention four areas in particular and perhaps you can relate to one or two, or maybe all four. Whatever they are, release is brought into each area in the same way.

First, acknowledge the bondage and where it has originated from, ie, Adam and Eve's sin, or through words spoken or read.

Second, repent of whatever it was that initially brought that bondage into your life. However it entered, we allowed it to become part of us.

Third, renounce ownership of the bondage. 'I no longer will live under this bondage. I believe that

Jesus Christ died upon the cross and shed His blood in order to redeem me from all that has come into my life as a consequence of Adam and Eve's sin. I disown its hold upon my life and I renounce it in the name of Jesus Christ. In Jesus Christ I have the right as a Son of God to be free from this bondage. I confess that it is no longer my problem.'

Fourth, we must resist every effort of Satan's to put us back into that bondage.

Remember that one of the definitions of the word 'curse' included the idea of being powerless to resist. Once the consequences of the curse of death have been broken in your life you will have the power to resist being brought back into the same bondage again.

Maintaining freedom

One of the ways to resist Satan is to take the example of Jesus Christ and to stand firmly upon the word of God.

James 4:7 tells us to submit ourselves to God and to resist the Devil and he will flee from us. Note that the first step is to submit ourselves to God. We will never be able to resist Satan in our own strength or ability; we will only have the power to resist him when we first stand upon God's Word. Standing upon, quoting, and truly believing the Word of God gives us a base from which to resist.

Submitting to God is submitting to what His Word has to say about us, then allowing that Word to become a part of us, so that we believe the Word of God rather than the negative words and seeds that have been part of our lives.

There is one powerful weapon which God has given us against Satan—our own will. Obviously the most powerful weapon is the name of the Lord Jesus Christ, but next to that lies our will and using that will to make a decision to say 'No.'

'No' is often referred to as the most powerful word we can express. Jesus, when He was tempted of the Devil in the wilderness, not only came against him with the Word of God, He also used His own will to resist the temptation.

I trust that you have been able to hear the voice of God speaking to you as you have read this book. It is my desire that each of you will be able to work this into your lives and live in victory.